diary of An Entrepreneur

DsWalker

"Failure will never overtake me if my determination
to succeed is strong enough"- Og Mandingo

The moment I failed is the moment I begin to succeed
and walk in my purpose.
I have felt the pain of failure and used that
feeling to succeed! My determination to win was at a whole
new level as I spoke success into my life.

About The Author

Dionna Walker was born, raised, and currently resides in Dayton, Ohio where she is a mother, wife, sister and devoted woman of God! She is currently working towards her degree in Social Work because she has a passion for advocating and working closely with children in need. She is no stranger to giving back and being an integral part of the Dayton community and beyond.

Her passions throughout her life have led her to become the founder of Dionna Helping Hands. Dionna Helping Hands is a non-profit organization that began in September 2015 in the city of Dayton, Ohio that provides free clothing and furniture as well as other assistances to families in need. Dionna's organization inspires and encourages love, peace and hope. She is also the proud founder of A Risen Queen empowerment clothing line which inspires women to stay motivated.

In addition to her giving heart and soul, she is a published author, who in 2014, received the honorable Dayton Book Expo Top Fiction Seller Award. Dionna was awarded the "Image of Hope "youth advocate" Award in Dayton, Ohio.

CONTENTS

DIARY OF AN ENTREPRENEUR

DS WALKER

CHAPTER

1 Business Building 1

2 Who Is Your Support System? 2

3 Stepping Out On Faith 4

4 Finding Your Free Space 6

5 The Moment You Give Up Is The Moment You Fail 7

6 Gaining Confidence While Building Your Business 9

7 The Only Person Holding You Back Is Yourself 11

8 Determination 13

9 Getting The Job Done 15

10 Dealing With The Word "No" 17

11 Social Media 19

12 Developing Your Pitch 21

13 Building Your Email List 23

14 Business License 24

Entrepreneur Diary 26

1
Business Building

Many people want to become an entrepreneur but only few recognize early that building a business can cause an increasing amount of stress. The beginner entrepreneur has no clue where to start and at times, seeks the advice of seasoned entrepreneurs. However, an average seasoned entrepreneur may not or will not share resources or give advice, fearful that you may succeed beyond them. Many entrepreneurs start a business for a chance at career freedom or to become the master of their own destinies. Others are looking for alternative income opportunities to supplement their already existing careers and/or life.

Your purpose is the reason why you exist it's the reason for being. Finding your life's purpose is very much about finding yourself. Life with a purpose drives you when you wake up each morning!

Do you believe that starting your own business is your life purpose? Can you see yourself doing this your entire Life?

Below are 5 questions to help you think more about your life purpose. Answer the questions after thoughtfully pondering them.

1. What kind of person are you?

2. What do you love to do?

3. What are some reason behind why you do what you do?

4. What do you want or need to be successful?

5. How do you think success would change you?

2
Who Is Your Support System?

Not everyone can or will understand your passion in your business. Not everyone will support you! It's vital to figure out who your supporters are. A supporter will be there to offer you great advice. He or she is not afraid to let you know when you are wrong and will tell you the truth despite your feelings. This person will go the extra mile to help you succeed. If you s urround yourself around followers, please make room for your supporters.

Here are a few questions that can help you identify your support system.
1.   Are you surrounding yourself around positive energy?
2.   Can you identify positive energy in your life?
3.   Are you surrounding yourself around positive people?
4.   Who are the positive people in your life?
5.   Can you identify the positive people in your life?
6.   How are they impacting you to become better?
7.   Who is your support system?

Surround yourself around people that will help you reach your goals in your life whether big or small. Find people that are already in positions where you want to be and not around people that have never accomplished anything or who aren't going anywhere. Surround yourself around people that have made accomplishments and going somewhere in life.

My number one supporter is my husband. He is always in my corner cheering me on whenever I want to give up. He pushes me to continue because he knows what I do is my true passion.

Write down five people who will support you no matter win or lose. These people are not afraid to tell you when you're wrong and are there to help you development.

1.

2.

3.

4.

5.

When things aren't going well or when you are just not feeling that great, support and encouragement is a necessity. For those who try to tough it alone, it can be a difficult, uphill battle. I recommend finding a mentor who has a lot of wisdom, experience and insight. This can also be found in friends, family or colleagues who have experienced running a business first-hand. My family members have several businesses in the Ohio area. I took my own advice and learned from the people literally closest to me.

Before we get to the point of great difficulty, which is when you want to give up or are feeling overwhelmed to the point of quitting, or in anticipation of life's little setbacks, we should implement strategies or have a support system in place to help us through some of those rough spots.

Here are some tips:
- Turn to family members and friends.
- Cultivate a variety of interests.
- Get into the gym and exercise and play sports.
- Take a short, affordable trip that fits your budget.
- Create a quiet place or sanctuary for yourself.
- Volunteer at a local nonprofit organization.

3
Stepping Out On Faith

"Getting off the ground is the easy part.
Stepping out on faith is the hardest."

The moment you learn to take your first steps as a child or learn how to drive or take the train, you have stepped out on faith. We step out on faith each and every time we cook a new meal, agree to go on a first date, or apply for a new job. We never know how these things will turn out but we do it anyway, regardless of the consequences. So, why not step out on faith to build your empire?

Let me tell you! Some people are afraid of change or something new. They are afraid to let go and take a chance. There is great power in not knowing what happens next. The moment I decided to leave my job and stop helping build someone else's empire, I began to walk into my purpose. Are you determined to secure the future you want to live? Are you ready to step out on faith?

What is "Speaking into existence?"

When you claim greatness into existence over your life, you're claiming good things to happen. Maybe you are seeking a new job, car, house or even a marriage. Claiming good things over your life helps put positive vibes out into the universe. Everything I speak out into the universe becomes mine. Speak good over your life! There are enough people doubting you and your abilities so always speak greatness over your life. Speaking this into existence is just the first step. You must take action and work hard to secure the lifestyle you want to live. This requires much determination.

Stepping out on faith and taking a risk can be fearful and scary but sometimes you just have to go for it.

Here are three simple questions that helped me step out on faith.

1. Are you worried about paying bills? Great! Step out on faith.
One day I was in my tub thinking about what people would say about me at my funeral and what I had done worth remembering? Then, I focused my attention on all the great things I wanted to do. That's when, day-by-day, I began to not worry about bills or money. I decided to step out on faith and began to do what I wanted with no hesitation.

2. Are you worried about how you're going to send your kids to college? Good! Step out on faith. What are you doing today to secure your children's futures? When given the opportunity to work extra hours or gain increases in income, do you take it? For every penny you earn, 10% of it should go toward your children's future! Stop worrying and step out on faith!

3. Tired of your boss treating you like crap? Wonderful. Step out on faith. Many people live life doing just enough to get by, which can lead to a very miserable future. You should always want more. Never feel obligated to stay in a situation just because you are barely getting by.

As I stated earlier, speaking good over my life wasn't enough. Stepping out on faith and applying myself was what I needed too. My determination to win was now at a whole new level as I spoke success into my life.

So.......

If you want a new job, speak it into existence.

If you want a fast new car, speak it into existence.

If you want to find a husband or wife, speak it into existence.

Always speak good things into your life.

4
Finding Your
Free Space

Do you have a space in your home where you can unwind, listen to music or even read a book? This area must be stress- and work-free. This is your calm place for meditation and prayer. Every day I take 25 minutes, in my free space, to pray and ask God for strength. I read in my free space and maybe drink a glass of wine while I relax. I do this sometimes during lunch or even after. I shut off my phone and really enjoy my quiet time.

Sometimes you get so caught up trying to build our empire that you forget to just take a moment to relax. Taking a moment to unwind can help you come up with businesses ideas or personal or professional goals.
Surrounding your free space with milestone you accomplished could be good for encouragements. I challenge you to take a moment out your day to just praise yourself for all your accomplishments.

Most business owners are very stressed and overwhelmed. They live hectic lives that can be altered at any given time. Relaxing can help you to not burn out. Find your free space and enjoy it.

5
The Moment You Give Up Is The Moment You Fail

The moment I failed was the moment I began to succeed. I began to walk in my purpose. I have felt the pain of failure and have used it to succeed. My determination to win is now at a whole new level. I spoke success into my life to help me towards my life's purpose. At times, I had high hopes for potential partnerships and sponsors but as in life, not everything works out and it was very hard to deal with. However, I didn't let that stop me. I worked harder and rearranged my business pitch and all over approach to continue to drive my business.

What is failure in business?
Business failure refers to a company not making money. A profitable business can fail if it does not generate adequate cash flow to meet expenses.

How can you prevent your business from failing?
Having great business management and planning will help your business from failing. If you don't know where to start, hire someone to help you build and plan for your business. Nowadays, people want to jump into things and not do any research first. Your business will live as long as you have a plan to keep building it.

Here are a few suggestions on how to avoid business failure.

1. Manage your cash flow.
Many startup businesses struggle with cash flow which is income your business makes.

2. Develop a strong business plan
Who is your target market? What type of business are you going into? Have you made 2-3 year goal for your business?

3. Avoid high debt.
Loans, credit cards and other forms of debt can be a double-edged sword for a small business. You have to make sure your business will recycle income before jumping into loans.

4. Make Accurate Projections.
Do your homework and find a mentor! Shadow a business like yours and learn from them. DO NOT COPY!

The cost of failure.

Business risks are influenced by numerous factors including sales volume, per-unit price, input costs, competition, the overall economic climate and government regulations. There is the possibility that your company will have lower than anticipated profits or experience a loss rather than taking a profit, especially in the initial few years. There are many risks to starting your own business so always remember that your business will go as far as you take it.

Here are three questions you should ask yourself about your potential business and failure.
1.   Are you determined to fail?
2.   Can you deal with failure?
3.   Once you fail, will you get back up?

6
Gaining Confidence While Building Your Business

I have worked with the top businesses and organizations in Dayton however, I began to question my abilities while being surrounded by such success. I wondered how I was able to achieve such a high place in my business with all these other businesses in operation. I then had to remind myself that I was in this position because of my hard work and dedication. I applied myself, just like everyone else, and I was in certain situations because of my accomplishments.

Ultimately, my confidence began to show through my public speeches and conversations. I often felt uncomfortable because I was surrounded by people with degrees and college experiences that assisted them to get to where they were. I felt like I couldn't carry on a conversation with college graduates without feeling stupid so I decided to go back to college myself. I didn't do this to prove something to anything to anyone but rather to make myself feel better about me.

How can you gain confidence?
1.   Package yourself for success
2.   Develop your brand
3.   Be a great communicator
4.   Look and act confident. When you look the part, you'll carry yourself with more confidence.
5.   Be physically active in all business aspects
6.   Do your best and worry less
7.   Let go of small mistakes.
8.   Continue to grow and improve.
9.   Write down your business goals and look at them daily.
10.   Be determined and negotiate fearlessly

Failure is an event, not a person, so always believe in yourself. Know when to focus and when to multitask. Having confidence in yourself, others, and in business is vital to your success. If you are thinking of starting a business or you already own a business, you must already have some self-confidence to take such a big risk.

7
The Only Person Holding You Back Is Yourself

Typically, the term procrastination carries a negative tone and is often used in describing delays. For me, procrastination means taking too much time to make the very best decisions for my business. Sometimes this will result in losing a partner or not meeting marketing deadlines. The amount of time you spend making a decision for your business operations could either benefit or defeat your goals. You always want to practice patience and discipline in business and never jump head first! Take your time and decide which business deal to take on first and then do not procrastinate.

What is procrastination?

How to identify procrastination?
Sometimes procrastination takes place until the last minute before a deadline needs to be met. It can take hold of any aspect of your life such as putting off cleaning the stove, repairing a leaky roof, or even visiting the doctor or dentist. It can also lead to feelings of guilt, inadequacy, depression and self-doubt.

To help procrastination, break large tasks down into smaller, more manageable ones. For example, the big task of getting new representation can seem overwhelming. Divide the workload and give yourself small, specific tasks with deadlines to help you create an action-oriented plan. One day you might research offices that are accepting submissions. The next day you might ask friends for referrals. The following day you compose your cover letter, and so on. Remind yourself that there's always more to be done than can be done. Always ask yourself if you're getting the most important things done before the least important.

Below are ways to avoid procrastination.

1. Stop Thinking Too Much
Stop wasting time thinking of all the things that could go wrong and just begin.

2. Prepare
Set daily goals for your business to accomplish them. If you need to create a Facebook business page, set a few hours aside to get it done. If you need printed material, hire someone.

3. Have Faith
Faith is taking the first step even when you don't see the whole staircase.

4. Set Goals
Goal setting is the first step in turning the invisible into visible.

5. Make A Decision
A day is made of hundreds of small decisions so don't agonize over what to do. Decisions force us to close the door on other possibilities and continue to move forward.

6. Face Your Fear
Never give up and continue to push forward.

7. Practice Taking The Next Step
Don't rush yourself, but do push yourself. Once you find you're able to handle the first step, continue to proceed full force.

Trust in your decision making.

If we continually question a decision, we can't move forward. Taking care of your business goals one step at a time will help you eliminate putting off work that needs to get done. I have found that creating a list of my daily goals has helped me not procrastinate or put things off for a later date.

8
Determination

What does determination mean to you? Do you believe that you are a determined person? Do you have the qualities to be and stay determined?

Determination is simply not giving up. No matter how hard things get, or how badly you want to just give up, you keep on going. Sometimes you just want to let go when it seems like what you're going for is just out of reach. Sometimes you tell yourself if what you're trying to get is worth the great amount of effort that you put in it. When things get hard, you start thinking that it's not worth it and that you just want to let it go but let me tell you this, the more pain and suffering you put into something, the better it'll feel when you accomplish the goal.

How to Gain Determination
Determination is inside all of us but we just have to find it. We must have the willpower to accomplish any and everything we set out to do.
Have you ever wanted something so bad as a child you talked about it all the time and ask your parents to buy it and you wouldn't let up until you receive it? That's what I call determination. I see it everyday with my children. Not letting up and asking for help to achieve your goals are required tasks. We all have practiced determination at some point in our lives so look deep and continue to be determined in whatever you are doing.

How To Use Determination
Determination is considered a laudable and coveted personality trait because it indicates that individuals are motivated to succeed, which translates to them getting tasks done and accomplishing goals.

Sacrifices of Determination

Determination means you look at yourself and you find no excuses. And when you find your strengths and weaknesses, you better utilize them and accomplish everything you have in mind with no excuses. If you fail, don't worry about it. Just get right back up and continue. If you don't fail, then you're not doing anything right and are afraid of failing. Failing is something you cannot ignore. It's something everyone comes across in life. That's why people learn from mistakes and move on.

9
Getting
The Job Done

I learned to listen to what a person didn't say and base my opinion of them off the things they left out.

Stop and consider for a moment reasons why you don't like someone. Maybe you think he or she is greedy and selfish. Or possibly, their dismissive nature to others and yourself can be downright mean. In other words, there are some character flaws or disagreeable traits in others that can bother and irritate you.

Can you get past these issues to get the job done? Learning to get past difficult people will keep you in business for a very long time. As a professional, you have to be able to handle yourself in difficult situations.

I typically go into a business partnership knowing the risks. I usually reach out to businesses I can help or receive help from. For me, each person I work with can add to my business rather than take away.

In business, your name is like credit. Businesses love doing credibility check. This is when someone ask around about you in regards to your personality, business partnerships, ethics, and many more. Do you have good credit? Getting into a relationship with businesses that don't have a credit can hurt your new business. Tread lightly when you partner with other businesses. Always do your homework! During my first year of my business, before I jumped into a partnership, I did my homework. I only had 3 partners with other organizations. Each partnership brought different things to the table that I couldn't provide. about the businesses you are trying to partner with.

Never allow negative feelings get in the way of you achieving your goals. Sometimes you just have to bite the bullet, stay determined, and go after your goals.

I really had to accept the fact that I wasn't the know-it-all that I thought I was. Reaching out to these individuals and accepting I couldn't do it all was a major step in my business development. Now, not only are things running a lot more smoothly for my business, but I have helped other businesses reach their goals, gain exposure and build new partnerships.

Not blaming yourself or feeling down because of a partnership or business deal didn't work out is very important. Learn from it and apply the changes to your next business deal. Sometimes it's not your fault. Maybe the business you're partnering with could have issues with your business or getting into a partnership all together. Just be aware and learn as much as you can.

10
Dealing With
The Word "No"

If you deal with rejection personally, you'll struggle to grow your business.

If you can get past the possibilities of a rejection from a potential date, job opportunity, bank, or business deal, then you can look at every "no" as one step closer to that "yes". Instead of getting defeated by rejection, learn to see it as just one step on the path to your ultimate goal.

Received a rejection? Ask questions regarding the decision. Sample questions can include "Can you share advice on how I can improve my business proposal?" and "Why is my business not a good fit for your business?" Listen carefully to their responses and encourage them to be completely honest with their feedback. One of the most important things to do in business is to listen and learn to ask questions. Ultimately, thank the person or company for their time and consideration and leave on a positive note.

Once you have taken their feedback into consideration, assess any problem areas and make changes within your business and adjust your approach as needed. You'll likely find that you get fewer "no's" and more "yeses" however rejection can be hard. No one likes to be rejected. Rejection will never disappear without making necessary adjustments. Facing rejection doesn't make you a failure but failing to learn from them just might! However, a "no" can mean "I don't know?" or "I'm not ready at the moment." and in these type of situations, leave your contact information and thank them.

I remember one time, a business swore against accepting new clients. However, by the end of the week, the business called and offered us a business partnership and we were added to their list and moved ahead of every other business. How did I do it?

I left the meeting asking and answering questions. I also left my contact information behind so they could contact me. Never leave a stone unturned.

Ask Questions
- "Why can't we work together?"
- "Does my business not fit into your business partnership agendas?"
- " Do you see something within my business plan that worries you?"

Leave Contact Information
- Leaving a business card behind is not only professional, but a great way to easily provide information about yourself without coming off aggressive.

Maturity is when you realize that getting rejected isn't always a bad thing. I am thankful for every employer that said no to me. It is my prayer that I walk into all that I am called to be and do so that I can turn around and be a financial blessing to others. I am thankful for the rejections. Embrace your failures as one step closer to accomplishing your goals! Don't take rejection as you if you have failed. Make changes and apply it to your business so it can continue to grow.

Always be prepared for the possibility of a no. If you are, then you will do the follow:
1. Leave your contact information
2. Ask questions
3. Learn from your mistakes
4. Take into consideration the answers you received from asking why the company didn't want to do business with you.
5. Work on your deliverance.
6. Prepare for better business opportunities.

Having the right attitude about a "no" can really go a long way. It can actually get you closer to getting a "yes". You must fail in order to win. In business, you might get a 100 "no's" but once you get that one "yes", you will feel more successful today then you were yesterday!

Remember to ask questions when faced with rejection. Ask yourself, "What can I do to secure the next business deal?" If you hear "no" a lot, it's probably a hint to fix something with your strategies. Always ask questions to know what to fix and update for the next time. Always learn from feedback, apply it, and get back out there.

11
Social Media

Top five ways social media helped my business!

Social Media
1. GRAPHIC DESIGNER- Graphic designing has become a part of every industry. Graphic designers produce the visual media that business need to brand, promote and market. Hiring a good graphic designer is key to success so make sure you do your research. Once you find your designer, begin to design your logo. This will get the attention of customers and
potential business partners.

Branding
BRAND vs. Branding
2. Brand is not branding. The difference between brand and branding is that one is a marketing tool and the other is an action. Branding is about defining, while advertising is about promoting. A brand is a person's
emotional response -a gut feeling about an organization, a product, or a service. In essence, your customers own your brand, you do not. You don't have direct control of the perceptions held by customers.

Branding is not about stamping a trademark on everything, but guiding and managing relationships with your customers. You're branding yourself right now as an individual part of the family collective and your business. Realize that you only have partial control of the perceptions with your branding activities.

Facebook
3. Create your Facebook business page and include information about your business, mission and services you provide. Encourage friends and family to share and like your page. Introduce your business to other organizations or businesses online and like their stuff.

My daily goals for Facebook are to share my business page 3 times a day in the morning, at lunch, and around dinnertime. I did the routine for 6 months and received 7 new follower a day. Facebook shouldn't be your only marketing platform. Donors and sponsors will not take you seriously if this is your only source to the world. Get up and Get off "the book."

Website Development
4. Find a company that will develop a website that will cater to your business needs and express your target audience to them.

Make sure your website is:
1. Sleek
2. Modern
3. Safe and secure
4. Include details about the business and owner
5. Blogging - This is a great way to keep traffic coming to your website

Make sure you upkeep your website. This is essential. Customers hate a complicated website. If you become to busy to maintain your website, hire help!

Handwrite Letters
5. People never really handwrite letters now a days. With all the different forms of communication like apps and texting, who has time to write a well-written, signed and sealed letter? We received a response from each hand-written letter we sent. Some responses were good while some were bad! But we did it!

Personal Phone Calls
6. Social media Shouldn't be your only connection you have to your customers. Yes! I make follow up phone calls and send text messages. Sometimes people just need that extra push to seal the deal.

 I LOVE social media but it's not my only Marketing platform. As an Entrepreneur we must use every trick in the book. I love using old school marketing tools to promote my business. Here are a few: Phone Calls, Billboards, Public Transportation, and Handwritten Letters.

Do what you must to reach your Target Market.
What happens to your business if social media crash?

12
Developing
Your Pitch

"Everyone wants to live on top of the mountains, but all the happiness and growth occurs while you're climbing it."

Your business pitch is a presentation by one or more people to an investor or group of investors. You will not get good at pitching unless you experience it first-hand. No one can prepare you for what investors might do or say unless of course, you're psychic! Each business situation is different and you don't want to cheat yourself or your business! Develop your pitch based on your needs to gain investors. Before you pitch your business to an investor, you must develop what you need and why this investor should help you.

During my very first pitch, I was unsure of myself and my business needs. My body language and presentation showed just how naive and unprepared I was. Investors hate to have their time wasted. Take time to prepare your pitch for your business and do your homework for investors. Google will be your best friend as you search for how to create your pitch and on your search for an investor. It is worth your time!

This is the part of the book where I have to just tell it like it is!

You can't practice a pitch! Why you ask? Well, every investor is different. One investor might like a video presentation and will you be prepared if all you brought was a graph and outline to the meeting? Learn what your investors like and even if you have to, research the business and call and ask the assistant or secretary for help. Do your homework!

You can practice a million times but that will not help if your investor is not interested in what you're pitching! Trust me, they have heard it all before. Investors want you to tell them why you want their money!

This is your chance to sell your business to an investor. Make sure you know how to approach the situation. I'm not suggesting for you to not develop a pitch. I'm suggesting you make sure your pitch is suitable for different types of situations!

Step to developing a perfect pitch!
1. Know exactly what you want and need from investors! Be very upfront about your intentions.

2. Why is your business worth investing in? At this point you should describe your business as if it's the last business on Earth.

3. Always prepare to explain your business to any audience.

13
Building
Your Email List

Why You Should Start Building an Email List?

Aside from your website, your Email List is 100 percent under your control. Social media is essential to growing a profitable Business. But what happens to your business if social media crash? you'll still have an email list full of dedicated followers who are there to open your emails and read your most important updates.

Do you ever intend to sell products or services on your website? Then you need an email list. EMAIL SUBSCRIBERS ARE MORE LIKELY TO BE PRODUCT BUYERS. Building your email list will allow you to send them emails. If someone subscribed to your email list they like you and mean business. they might just want whatever it is that you're selling.

Email Listing is the easiest way to share big announcements and keeping in touch. Every customer can't check your social media every day. But what will they do? they'll probably check their email every day. if you have something important to share, then an email list is an excellent medium to keep in touch.

I think business owners should be trying to grow their email list, especially if you intend to sell products or services of any kind.

14
Business License

Many new business owners think that forming an LLC or corporation is the same as getting a business license. Then unfortunately, some realize this isn't the case when they are fined for operating without a license.

A business license gives you the right to operate. Think of it this way: getting an LLC is the first step and creates a legal foundation for the business. A business license gives you the right to operate. Depending on what kind of business you have and where you live, you may need to get business licenses from your state, county, or town.

Examples include: zoning permit, permit from the health department, professional licenses, a general business operation license, and home occupation permits. Most licenses are relatively inexpensive and getting one upfront will save you money and keep your business legit. Check with your local board of equalization offices, or find a service to determine which permits your business needs to legally operate.

Many states require what is called a seller's permit. THIS permit is required for sole proprietors, LLCs, partnerships, and corporations that sell taxable goods and services. I get so many questions about an EIN also known as a federal tax ID number, this is a way for the IRS to identify your business and track its transactions. Think of an EIN like a social security number for companies. If you plan on having employees, an EIN is mandatory.

This is very important please Insure Your Business
While forming an LLC or incorporating does help protect your personal assets from any liability of the company, it doesn't protect the business itself from losses. That's why you should consider getting a general liability insurance or a Business Owners Policy (BOP).

These policies will broadly cover your business against accidents, injuries, and negligence claims.

Make a plan to keep your LLC compliant. you've got to operate your business at a higher administrative level than you've been used to as a sole proprietor. Both LLCs and corporations often need to file an annual report with their state, as well as keep up with their quarterly tax payments. Mark these important dates on a calendar ahead of time, or sign up for a service that will automatically send you alerts ahead of key state and federal filing deadline.

Entrepreneur Diary

This book details steps I took to eliminate stress from my life and business. I pray that this diary helps you on your journey to success!

I challenge you to stay open to your own thoughts and how they impact your feelings towards learning more about your life's purpose.

I Dare you to acknowledge any negative energy as a source to positive energy.

I Dare you to be bold and confident. This diary is for you to create your very own Journey to success.

Date:

Affirmation:

Who or what inspired you today?

Goals:

Business	Personal	Weekly

Weekly Quote:

What's On Your Mind?

Date:

Affirmation:

Who or what inspired you today?

Goals:

Business	Personal	Weekly

Weekly Quote:

Date:

Affirmation:

Who or what inspired you today?

Goals:

Business	Personal	Weekly

Weekly Quote:

What's On Your Mind?

Date:

Affirmation:

Who or what inspired you today?

Goals:

Business	Personal	Weekly

Weekly Quote:

Date:

Affirmation:

Who or what inspired you today?

Goals:

Business	Personal	Weekly

Weekly Quote:

What's On Your Mind?

Date:

Affirmation:

Who or what inspired you today?

Goals:

Business	Personal	Weekly

Weekly Quote:

Date:

Affirmation:

Who or what inspired you today?

Goals:

Business	Personal	Weekly

Weekly Quote:

What's On Your Mind?

Date:

Affirmation:

Who or what inspired you today?

Goals:

Business	Personal	Weekly

Weekly Quote:

Date:

Affirmation:

Who or what inspired you today?

Goals:

Business	Personal	Weekly

Weekly Quote:

What's On Your Mind?

Date:

Affirmation:

Who or what inspired you today?

Goals:

Business   Personal   Weekly

Weekly Quote:

Date:

Affirmation:

Who or what inspired you today?

Goals:

Business	Personal	Weekly

Weekly Quote:

What's On Your Mind?

Date:

Affirmation:

Who or what inspired you today?

Goals:

Business	Personal	Weekly

Weekly Quote:

Date:

Affirmation:

Who or what inspired you today?

Goals:

Business	Personal	Weekly

Weekly Quote:

What's On Your Mind?

Date:

Affirmation:

Who or what inspired you today?

Goals:

Business	Personal	Weekly

Weekly Quote:

Date:

Affirmation:

Who or what inspired you today?

Goals:

Business	Personal	Weekly

Weekly Quote:

What's On Your Mind?

Date:

Affirmation:

Who or what inspired you today?

Goals:

Business	Personal	Weekly

Weekly Quote:

Date:

Affirmation:

Who or what inspired you today?

Goals:

Business   Personal   Weekly

Weekly Quote:

What's On Your Mind?

Date:

Affirmation:

Who or what inspired you today?

Goals:

Business   Personal   Weekly

Weekly Quote:

Date:

Affirmation:

Who or what inspired you today?

Goals:

Business   Personal   Weekly

Weekly Quote:

What's On Your Mind?

Date:

Affirmation:

Who or what inspired you today?

Goals:

Business	Personal	Weekly

Weekly Quote:

Date:

Affirmation:

Who or what inspired you today?

Goals:

Business	Personal	Weekly

Weekly Quote:

What's On Your Mind?

Date:

Affirmation:

Who or what inspired you today?

Goals:

Business	Personal	Weekly

Weekly Quote:

Date:

Affirmation:

Who or what inspired you today?

Goals:

Business	Personal	Weekly

Weekly Quote:

What's On Your Mind?

Date:

Affirmation:

Who or what inspired you today?

Goals:

Business	Personal	Weekly

Weekly Quote:

Date:

Affirmation:

Who or what inspired you today?

Goals:

Business	Personal	Weekly

Weekly Quote:

What's On Your Mind?

Date:

Affirmation:

Who or what inspired you today?

Goals:

Business	Personal	Weekly

Weekly Quote:

Date:

Affirmation:

Who or what inspired you today?

Goals:

Business	Personal	Weekly

Weekly Quote:

What's On Your Mind?

Date:

Affirmation:

Who or what inspired you today?

Goals:

Business	Personal	Weekly

Weekly Quote:

Date:

Affirmation:

Who or what inspired you today?

Goals:

Business	Personal	Weekly

Weekly Quote:

What's On Your Mind?

Date:

Affirmation:

Who or what inspired you today?

Goals:

Business   Personal   Weekly

Weekly Quote:

Date:

Affirmation:

Who or what inspired you today?

Goals:

Business   Personal   Weekly

Weekly Quote:

What's On Your Mind?

Date:

Affirmation:

Who or what inspired you today?

Goals:

Business	Personal	Weekly

Weekly Quote:

Date:

Affirmation:

Who or what inspired you today?

Goals:

Business	Personal	Weekly

Weekly Quote:

What's On Your Mind?

Date:

Affirmation:

Who or what inspired you today?

Goals:

Business	Personal	Weekly

Weekly Quote:

Date:

Affirmation:

Who or what inspired you today?

Goals:

Business	Personal	Weekly

Weekly Quote:

What's On Your Mind?

Date:

Affirmation:

Who or what inspired you today?

Goals:

Business	Personal	Weekly

Weekly Quote:

Date:

Affirmation:

Who or what inspired you today?

Goals:

Business	Personal	Weekly

Weekly Quote:

What's On Your Mind?

Date:

Affirmation:

Who or what inspired you today?

Goals:

Business	Personal	Weekly

Weekly Quote:

Date:

Affirmation:

Who or what inspired you today?

Goals:

Business	Personal	Weekly

Weekly Quote:

What's On Your Mind?

Date:

Affirmation:

Who or what inspired you today?

Goals:

Business	Personal	Weekly

Weekly Quote:

Date:

Affirmation:

Who or what inspired you today?

Goals:

Business	Personal	Weekly

Weekly Quote:

What's On Your Mind?

Date:

Affirmation:

Who or what inspired you today?

Goals:

Business	Personal	Weekly

Weekly Quote:

Date:

Affirmation:

Who or what inspired you today?

Goals:

Business	Personal	Weekly

Weekly Quote:

What's On Your Mind?

Date:

Affirmation:

Who or what inspired you today?

Goals:

Business	Personal	Weekly

Weekly Quote:

Date:

Affirmation:

Who or what inspired you today?

Goals:

Business	Personal	Weekly

Weekly Quote:

What's On Your Mind?

Date:

Affirmation:

Who or what inspired you today?

Goals:

Business	Personal	Weekly

Weekly Quote:

Date:

Affirmation:

Who or what inspired you today?

Goals:

Business	Personal	Weekly

Weekly Quote:

What's On Your Mind?

Date:

Affirmation:

Who or what inspired you today?

Goals:

Business	Personal	Weekly

Weekly Quote:

Date:

Affirmation:

Who or what inspired you today?

Goals:

Business	Personal	Weekly

Weekly Quote:

What's On Your Mind?

Date:

Affirmation:

Who or what inspired you today?

Goals:

Business	Personal	Weekly

Weekly Quote:

Date:

Affirmation:

Who or what inspired you today?

Goals:

Business	Personal	Weekly

Weekly Quote:

What's On Your Mind?

Date:

Affirmation:

Who or what inspired you today?

Goals:

Business	Personal	Weekly

Weekly Quote:

Date:

Affirmation:

Who or what inspired you today?

Goals:

Business	Personal	Weekly

Weekly Quote:

What's On Your Mind?

Date:

Affirmation:

Who or what inspired you today?

Goals:

Business	Personal	Weekly

Weekly Quote:

Date:

Affirmation:

Who or what inspired you today?

Goals:

Business	Personal	Weekly

Weekly Quote:

What's On Your Mind?

Date:

Affirmation:

Who or what inspired you today?

Goals:

Business	Personal	Weekly

Weekly Quote:

Date:

Affirmation:

Who or what inspired you today?

Goals:

Business	Personal	Weekly

Weekly Quote:

What's On Your Mind?

Date:

Affirmation:

Who or what inspired you today?

Goals:

Business	Personal	Weekly

Weekly Quote:

Date:

Affirmation:

Who or what inspired you today?

Goals:

Business	Personal	Weekly

Weekly Quote:

What's On Your Mind?

Date:

Affirmation:

Who or what inspired you today?

Goals:

Business	Personal	Weekly

Weekly Quote:

Date:

Affirmation:

Who or what inspired you today?

Goals:

Business	Personal	Weekly

Weekly Quote:

What's On Your Mind?

Date:

Affirmation:

Who or what inspired you today?

Goals:

Business	Personal	Weekly

Weekly Quote:

Date:

Affirmation:

Who or what inspired you today?

Goals:

Business	Personal	Weekly

Weekly Quote:

What's On Your Mind?

Date:

Affirmation:

Who or what inspired you today?

Goals:

Business	Personal	Weekly

Weekly Quote:

Date:

Affirmation:

Who or what inspired you today?

Goals:

Business	Personal	Weekly

Weekly Quote:

What's On Your Mind?

Date:

Affirmation:

Who or what inspired you today?

Goals:

Business   Personal   Weekly

Weekly Quote:

Date:

Affirmation:

Who or what inspired you today?

Goals:

Business	Personal	Weekly

Weekly Quote:

What's On Your Mind?

Date:

Affirmation:

Who or what inspired you today?

Goals:

Business	Personal	Weekly

Weekly Quote:

Date:

Affirmation:

Who or what inspired you today?

Goals:

Business	Personal	Weekly

Weekly Quote:

What's On Your Mind?

Date:

Affirmation:

Who or what inspired you today?

Goals:

Business	Personal	Weekly

Weekly Quote:

Date:

Affirmation:

Who or what inspired you today?

Goals:

Business	Personal	Weekly

Weekly Quote:

What's On Your Mind?

Date:

Affirmation:

Who or what inspired you today?

Goals:

Business	Personal	Weekly

Weekly Quote:

Date:

Affirmation:

Who or what inspired you today?

Goals:

Business	Personal	Weekly

Weekly Quote:

What's On Your Mind?

Date:

Affirmation:

Who or what inspired you today?

Goals:

Business	Personal	Weekly

Weekly Quote:

Date:

Affirmation:

Who or what inspired you today?

Goals:

Business   Personal   Weekly

Weekly Quote:

What's On Your Mind?

Date:

Affirmation:

Who or what inspired you today?

Goals:

Business	Personal	Weekly

Weekly Quote:

Date:

Affirmation:

Who or what inspired you today?

Goals:

Business	Personal	Weekly

Weekly Quote:

What's On Your Mind?

Date:

Affirmation:

Who or what inspired you today?

Goals:

Business	Personal	Weekly

Weekly Quote:

Date:

Affirmation:

Who or what inspired you today?

Goals:

Business	Personal	Weekly

Weekly Quote:

What's On Your Mind?

Date:

Affirmation:

Who or what inspired you today?

Goals:

Business   Personal   Weekly

Weekly Quote:

www.ingramcontent.com/pod-product-compliance
Lightning Source LLC
Chambersburg PA
CBHW071420180526
45170CB00001B/162